GoodNewzDudez
Presents:

TRAGEDY BRINGS TOGETHERNESS

written by Fred Robinson Jr

original characters by Gary James

Illustrated by Courtney Monday

i

This story takes place in Homestead, FL after hurricane Andrew hit the coast, in 1992. Members of the Good Newz Dudez; Globey, Seddrick, Diffy and Jiffy, live together in a house that was totally demolished by the storm.

Jiffy

Globey

Seddrick

Diffy

2

What's a hurricane, you ask? Let me tell you what a hurricane is and how they are formed! A hurricane is a huge storm! It can be up to 600 miles across and have strong winds spinning in and up at speeds of 75 to 200 mph. Each hurricane usually lasts for over a week, moving 10-20 miles per hour over the open ocean. Hurricanes gather heat and energy through contact with warm ocean waters.

Hey kids, if you ever see a telephone pole and wires on the ground stay far away. They can hurt you! Go get help from a grown up, like your Mom or Dad!

4

The firemen arrive to help the Good Newz Dudez.

5

6

7

The Good Newz Dudez Volunteer Fire Fighters are hard at work to save the house.

9

Meanwhile, Sheddrick is helping Globey feel better at the Rescue Van.
Nobody has seen Diffy and Jiffy. So, Melissa gets worried.
Rescue Station 7
What happened to Diffy and Jiffy?

13

16

The Good Newz Dudez begin looking around the house for things they may be able to save...

17

Many of the Good Newz Dudez begin thinking about what they may be able to give to rebuild the house.

Thinking about the house...
My Uncle Chuckletow has a lumber yard. He would be more than happy to give us what we need.

Is there any food? I haven't eaten in a long time!

I've got food for everyone. Thanks to our family and friends.
Melissa

Melissa and Jiffy are enjoying the food. Which gets the attention of Flem Flam.

Alright Good Newz Dudez, let's do this!

23

25

Stinky Winky and Flem Flam have a not-so-safe idea to get the material up to the roof. They want to use a Teeter Totter.

28

Step aside my friend. I'm just the man for this job.

29

Down comes Flem Flam
on the Teeter Totter.

30

Flem Flam jumps on the end of the Teeter Totter. All the supplies go flying in the air.

Flem Flam is shocked...
Oh, my glory, we sent everything flying. But in the wrong direction!

The neighbor's on the other side of the Good Newz Dudez House got a surprise!
Hey, you guys didn't have to give us all these supplies. Gee thanks!
It's a miracle! God truly does pour you out blessings you won't have room enough to receive.

Meanwhile... Sunflower and Melissa are hard at work.

My Grandpa is a plumbing expert. He taught me to shift this, this way. And tuck this, that way...

34

Sunflower and Melissa do there best to fix the plumbing inside the house.

Are you sure it's supposed to be this way?

36

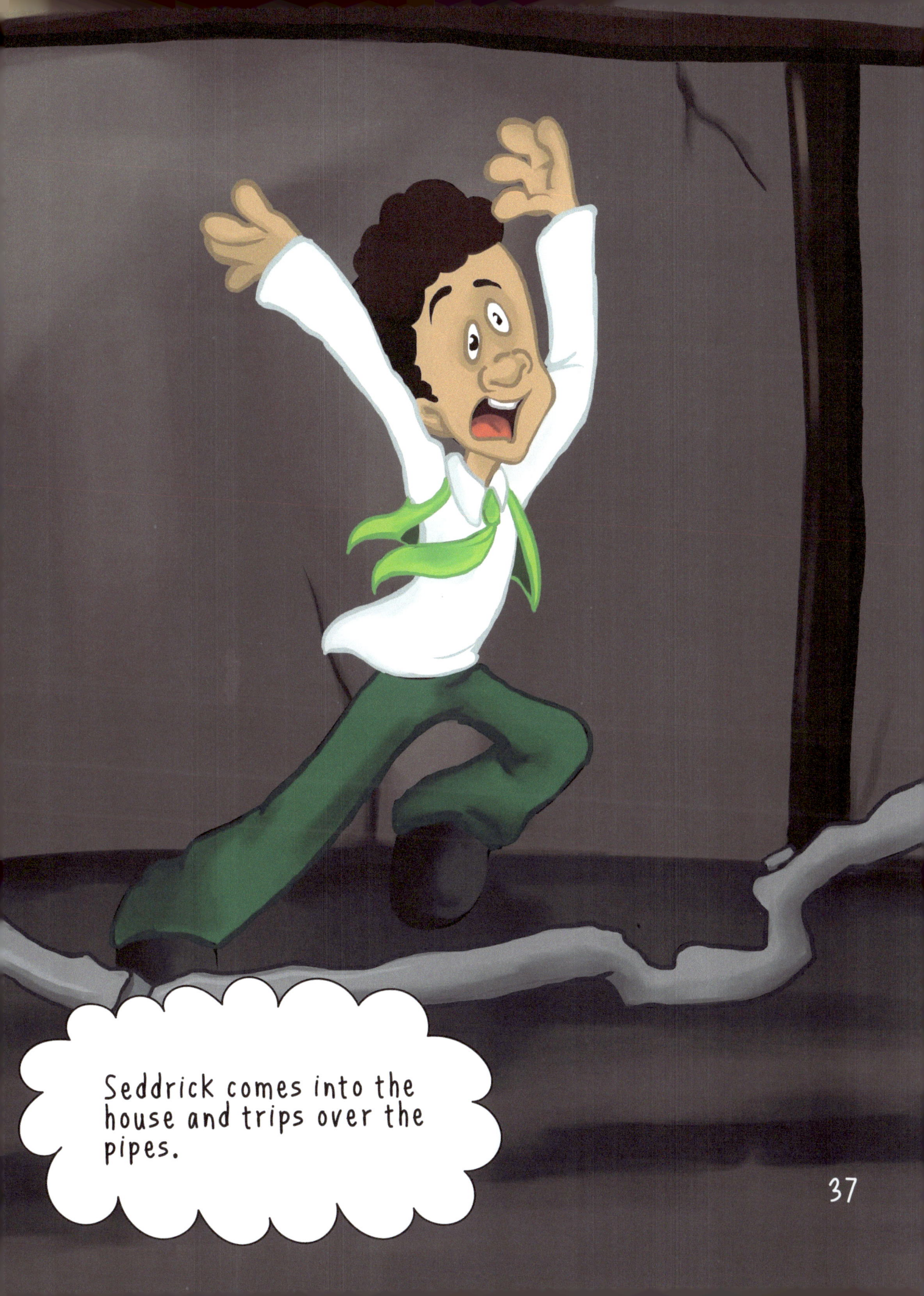

Seddrick comes into the house and trips over the pipes.

Seddrick's mistake is really a blessing. When he tripped over the pipes everything came together!
I didn't mean to mess up your work...
No problem, my brother
Yea, no problem

Melissa and Sunflower begin painting.

With the house nearly completed...
Almost finished!
Who said good things can't come out of a tragedy. We can do all things through Christ..."

You go Sunflower! I'm glad you are a Good Newz Dude! We learned that Bible lesson last year in school! Christ gives us strength to work together for the good of everyone.

Everyone is giving thanks to God for all the Good Newz Dudez working together!
You know guys, we really are blessed to be Good Newz Dudez!

44

Stinky Winky is marching around very happy everything turned out well. But, he's not really looking where he is going.

Stinky Winky steps on the bench where Melissa is sitting.

But, there is also a can of leftover paint on the bench. Into the air flies the paint and lands on the roof making a big mess. And onto the ground goes Melissa.

Stinky Winky feels bad about his mistake. Diffy and Jiffy run to give him a hug to help him feel better.

THE END

49

www.ingramcontent.com/pod-product-compliance
Lightning Source LLC
LaVergne TN
LVHW072053070426

835508LV00002B/78